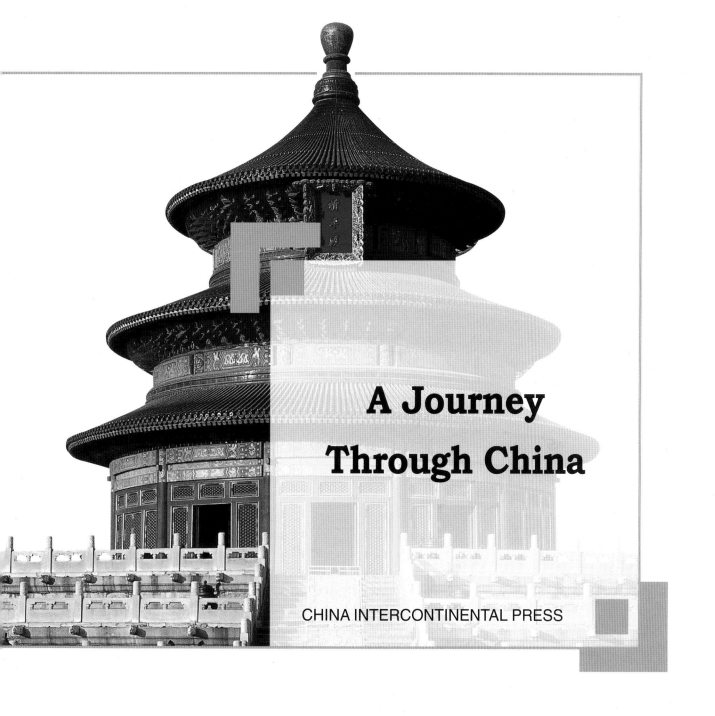

A Journey
Through China

CHINA INTERCONTINENTAL PRESS

China is a country of stunning landscapes and diverse ethnic and cultural traditions. Dramatic changes have occurred during the last twenty years of reform and opening, and visitors will discover a dynamic land that exceeds every expectation.

The Silk Road

The Silk Road unfolds like a paited scroll of China's cultural and historical legacies. Xi'an, the starting point of the Silk Road, is home to the Eighth Wonder of the World: the Terra Cotta Warriors and Horses buried more than 2,000 years ago in front of the Mausoleum of Emperor Qin Shihuang(221B.C.-206B.C.). At Dunhung, in northwest China's Gobi Desert, the Mogao Grottos (366-1368)are a lasting reminder of the cultural accomplishments of ancient Chinese peoples. Visitors can experience the awesome power of the Great Wall at Jiayuguan Pass, where the vast desert's ruins and relics offer a glimpse of the prosperous state of Loulan (300-420 A.D.)

China "Silk Road" Itinerary

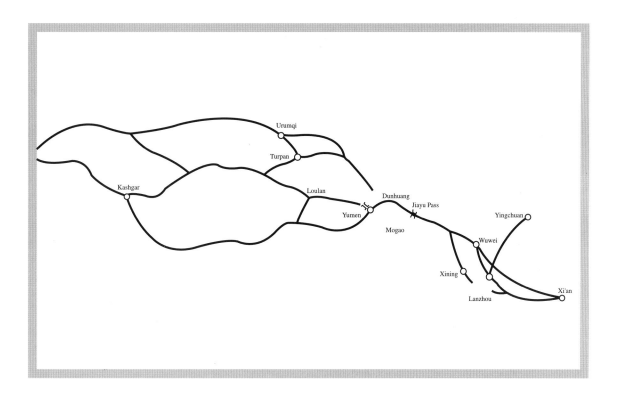

"Boats" in desert

Mausoleum of Kings of Xixia Kingdom in Ningxia

Charming river scene

Autumn

Elapsing time

Epitaph

Helanshan Mountain

Desolate desert

Ancient city of Ri Le of the Han Dynasty (206BC-220AD)

Remains of the Han Dynasty
beacon fire nearby Jianshuihou
Palace

Ruins of Heicheng on the Silk Road

Ruins of Shanmacheng

Ruins of Guangzhicheng

Yumenguan Pass at Pinghe

Ruins of Yangguan

Mogao Grottoes

Yueya Fountain

Jiayuguan Pass

Three Gorges of the Yellow River

Qinghai Lake

Tianchi Lake in Tianshan Mountain, Xinjiang

Grassland of Xinjiang

Murals at Dunhuang

Murals at Dunhuang

Folk Culture of Southwest China

The landscape of southwest China is a tapestry of boundless natural forest, lakes and rivers, highlands, canyons, and snow-capped mountains. Yunnan's Stone Forests and the Three Gorges of the Yangtze River are among the region's natural wonders that no visitor should miss.

Southwest China supports the nation's largest number of ethnic groups, whose diverse folk arts and customs can be best experienced during celebrations such as the Dai people's Water-Sprinkling Festival, the Tibetans' Shoton (Sour Milk Drinking) Festival, and the Torch Festival of the Yi people. Travelers will experience some of the country's most memorable accommodations in houses of 800 years old in Lijiang City, and find a version of ShangriLa in Zhongdian of Diqing.

Qutangxia Gorge of the Three Gorges of the Yangtze River

Xilingxia Gorge of the Three Gorges of the Yangtze River

Wuxia Gorge of the Three
Gorges of the Yangtze River

Qomolangmo

Giant statue of
Buddha in Leshan

Architecture unique to the Dong ethnic group in Guangxi

Tar Monastery in Qinghai

Tashilhunpo Monastery in Tibet

Potala Palace

Frescoes in the Potala Palace

Samye Monastery in Tibet

Women from Ngari in Tibet

Portrait of Buddha Unfolding Festival celebrated in the Zhaibung Monastery in Tibet

Lamas debating on the doctrines of Buddhist scripture.

Water Sprinkling Festival unique to the Dai ethnic group

An ancient town in Lijiang, Yunnan

Torch Festival unique to the Yi ethnic group

Singing Party of the Wa ethnic group

Bamboo houses of the Dai ethnic group

石林

Stone Forests in Yunnan

Presidential Journey

In 1998, US President Bill Clinton paid a State visit to China. His journey began in Beijing, where he admired the Forbidden City and climbed the Great Wall. He explored the dynamic Chinese city of Shanghai, chatted with farmers in suburban Xi'an, and contemplated the water scenes of Guilin, ending his tour at Hong Kong's Victorian Bay.

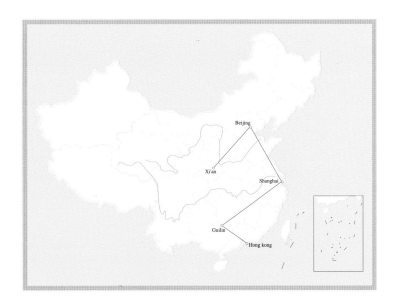

Great Wall

Tian An Men Gate in Beijing

Temple of Heaven

Palace Museum

64

Hall of Supreme Harmony

President Clinton visiting the Great Wall

President Clinton viewing Terra-cotta warriors and figures

Bund in Shanghai

Nanpu Bridge in Shanghai

Grand Theater at Yuyuan Garden in Shanghai

Guilin is known for having the most beautiful scenery in China

Lijiang River

Elephant Trunk Hill in Guilin

Lijiang River

Exhibition Center in Hong Kong

Victoria Harbor in Hong Kong

Southern China

Throughout Chinese history, area south of the Yangtze River has been known as a land of placid waterways and lush rice fields. The region's rich cultural traditions, exquisite gardens and architecture, and distinctive local produce and cuisine guarantee an unforgettable experience.

In Nanjing, the capital of of numerous ancient dynasties, tourists can trace a long history of beauty and wealth on both sides of the Qinhuai River. The legacies of Marco Polo linger on in the ancient city of Yangzhou, while Suzhou and Hangzhou have been described as earthly versions of paradise. Visitors will discover the charms of southern China in its lakes and rivers, its picturesque villages, and in the ordinary lives of its people.

Zhouzhuang, the number one of its kind
in area south of the Yangtze River

Zhouzhuang, the number one
of its kind in area south of the
Yangtze River

Taihu Lake in Wuxi in Jiangsu

Civilian housing in Wuxi in Jiangsu

Sailing boats on the Taihu Lake

Yihuan Garden in Wuxi in Jiangsu

Autumn Moon on the Calm Lake in
Hangzhou in Zhejiang

90

Hanshan Temple

Hall of Mahavira

Fengqiao Bridge

Embroidering girl in Suzhou

Sizilin Garden

Canglang Temple

Wangshi Garden

Qinhuai River

98

Langshan Mountain in Nantong

Heyuan in Yangzhou

中国旅游

顾　　问: 李冰　赵少华　李向平
主　　编: 郭长建
副 主 编: 宋坚之
责任编辑: 荆孝敏　汤贺伟
图片资料: 五洲传播出版社、深圳麟德电脑设计制作有限公司
封面设计: 杨津
版式设计: 宾峰

图书在版编目（CIP）数据

中国旅游: 英文/五洲传播出版社编.–北京: 五洲传播出版社,
2000.7
ISBN 7-80113-730-2
Ⅰ.中… Ⅱ.五… Ⅲ.名胜古迹–中国–摄影集 Ⅳ.K928.7-64
中国版本图书馆 CIP 数据核字（2000）第 65309 号

五洲传播出版社出版
社址: 中国北京北三环中路 31 号
邮政编码: 100083
电话: 010-62350055
网址: www.cicc.org.cn
深圳麟德电脑设计制作有限公司制版印刷
邮编: 518052
电话: 6641555 传真: 6641777
网址: www.luntak.com.cn
开本: 1/20
版次: 2000 年 7 月第一次版
印数: 1-2000
价格: 012000